THE
UNICORN GUIDE
to life

MAGICAL METHODS FOR LOOKING GOOD AND FEELING GREAT

EUNICE HORNE

Racehorse Publishing

To...

From...

INTRODUCTION

If you're currently living on Planet Earth, it can't have escaped your attention that unicorns are everywhere at the moment. For far too many years, these magical creatures frolicked and played in rainbow pastures just out of human sight, but recently, more and more of them have ventured into our world, in order to share their joy, mischief, and sparkle with us.

This little book is a guide to the unicorn way of life; in its chapters you'll learn about the unicorn philosophy, daily life, style, strength, and dreams, and by the time you reach the final page, you'll be ready to take on the world and make it more magical. You'll be charged with unicorn power from the tip of your glittery horn to the end of your swishy and sparkly tail.

Whether you're already a fully fledged unicorn fan, or a complete newcomer (also known as a "newnicorn") to the unicornverse, *The Unicorn Guide to Life* is here to teach you everything you ever dreamed of—and much, much more—about the marvelous, majestic and above all *magical* world of these miraculous creatures.

LIVING LA VIDA UNICORN

How to enjoy life as
much as unicorns do

BELIEVE IN MAGIC!

Have you ever wondered what puts the spring in a unicorn's step, or what gives a unicorn's horn that special rainbow sparkle? The answer is that all unicorns believe in magic. When you start believing, too, that's when your transformation into a magical unicorn will begin.

Magic comes in many different forms. There's the magic in hearing a baby's chuckle, stroking a puppy's soft silky fur, or simply having your bus turn up on time—with a free seat just waiting for you! Unicorns celebrate all these magical happenings, and the joy they find in them helps to bring even more wonder into their lives.

If I create from
the heart, nearly
everything works;
if from the head,
almost nothing.

—Marc Chagall

WHEN
SOMEBODY
TOLD ME I WAS
LIVING IN A
DREAM WORLD,
I NEARLY FELL OFF
MY UNICORN.

GIVE YOUR CREATIVITY FREE REIN

Picture a unicorn: what do you see? Some are quiet dreamers, conjuring up enchanting fairy stories in the shade of a tree, while others prance through the meadows, inviting all their friends to join them in a brand new game. Every unicorn has its own way of being in the world, but they are all united by their love of creativity. Whether you're a storyteller, a painter, a maker, or an organizer of the world's best parties, give yourself the time and space you need to bring your unique creative impulses to life, and share them with the world. That's real unicorn magic!

Everything you
can imagine
is real.

—Pablo Picasso

SPARKLE
WHEREVER
YOU GO.

BE INTERESTED IN THE WORLD AROUND YOU

Unicorns are always making new discoveries, because they love to look around corners, behind rain clouds, and into all sorts of other secret places where the magic of life takes place. That's how they found the end of the rainbow! Where will your explorations take you?

If you're not sure where to start, look at a travel timetable and plan a journey to somewhere you've never been. Take a bus, train, boat, or plane—unicorns love exploring and you never know what new places you'll discover, whether you're going to the other end of town or to a new continent!

Imagination is the highest kite one can fly.

—Lauren Bacall

LEARN SOMETHING NEW EVERY DAY

When you're a young child, your mind is always open, and learning is something you do as easily as breathing or blinking. But as we get older, the worlds of school and work can make learning feel like a bit of a chore—something we do *instead* of having fun.

Unicorns don't look at life this way: for a unicorn, every day is full of infinite possibility and learning is just one more way to explore the magic of the world. On a stormy day, when it's too dark and rainy for frolicking, our unicorn friends love to snuggle up indoors with a good book, because they know that knowledge has a special magic all of its own.

ALWAYS BE YOURSELF, UNLESS YOU CAN BE A UNICORN.

THEN
ALWAYS BE
A UNICORN.

Those who don't believe in magic will never find it.

—Roald Dahl

BE A UNICORN
IN A FIELD
OF HORSES.

EMBRACE ADVENTURES

Have you ever met a boring unicorn? Of course not. Every unicorn is born with an unquenchable spirit of adventure, and they never say no to an exciting new challenge or opportunity that comes their way.

The next time somebody invites you to try something new and you feel yourself pulling back into your comfort zone, ask yourself: what would a unicorn do? It could be that today is the day for you to begin your next new adventure.

Explore. Dream. Discover.

—H. Jackson Brown Jr

IS IT A STORM?
OR A CHANCE TO
PRANCE THROUGH
THE PUDDLES?

TAKE PLEASURE IN
THE EVERYDAY

Unicorns love to try new things, but what makes their lives truly magical is their ability to enjoy the delights of the everyday, just as much as breathtaking new experiences. When you open up your senses with a unicorn's playful approach to the world, you'll be startled at just how much joy can be found in the simple things of life.

When you're washing dishes, notice the softness of the bubbles, the scent of the steamy air and the smoothness of the clean warm plates. When you're walking down the street, feel the breeze caressing your face and revel in the sounds of nature and humankind that surround you. Just being fully present where you are right now is a kind of unicorn magic we can all achieve.

WORK, REST, AND PLAY THE UNICORN WAY

How to bring unicorn magic into your life from morning until night

GET PLENTY OF BEAUTY SLEEP

Unicorns feel great about the day ahead after a good night's sleep in the stable—getting plenty of rest is the secret beauty treatment that makes their rainbow sparkles shine even brighter and their multicolored tails swish even more extravagantly.

It's all too easy to stay up late watching the latest TV shows, or clicking through your favorite social media stream, but we all need peace and quiet before bedtime if we're going to get the most rest from our ZZZs. Be like a unicorn, and snuggle up peacefully for eight hours a night—the only question on your mind will be, "Where will my unicorn dreams take me tonight?"

A well-spent day brings happy sleep.

—Leonardo da Vinci

THERE'S MAGIC
INSIDE YOU.

GET YOUR GALLOP ON

Unicorns are known for bouncing through life with an endless supply of energy, and one reason for this is their love of activity. We all need a good rest when we're tired, but if you make the effort to bring some exercise in your life, you'll soon find that you have more vitality and that you're less eager to hit the sofa when you get the chance.

Exercise doesn't have to be a grind: be like a unicorn, and find a way of moving that brings you joy. You could prance through an aerobics class, trot round a netball pitch, canter on a running track, or fly down a zip wire with your mane streaming behind you. Once you find out that exercise is fun, you'll never look back!

Mix a little foolishness with your serious plans. It is lovely to be silly at the right moment.

—Horace

SWIM WITH
MERMAIDS, CHASE
RAINBOWS, PLAY
WITH FAIRIES, AND
RIDE A UNICORN.

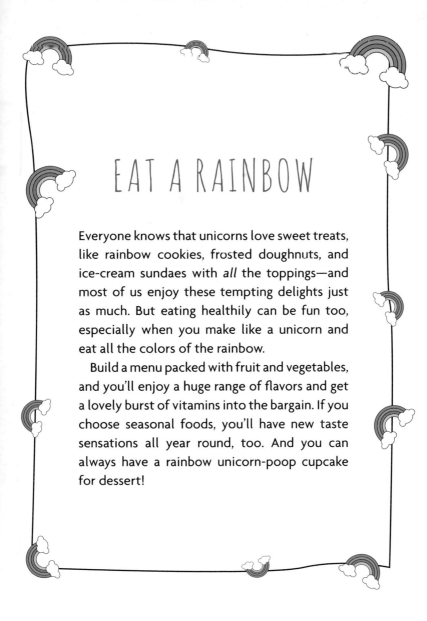

EAT A RAINBOW

Everyone knows that unicorns love sweet treats, like rainbow cookies, frosted doughnuts, and ice-cream sundaes with *all* the toppings—and most of us enjoy these tempting delights just as much. But eating healthily can be fun too, especially when you make like a unicorn and eat all the colors of the rainbow.

Build a menu packed with fruit and vegetables, and you'll enjoy a huge range of flavors and get a lovely burst of vitamins into the bargain. If you choose seasonal foods, you'll have new taste sensations all year round, too. And you can always have a rainbow unicorn-poop cupcake for dessert!

One cannot think
well, love well,
sleep well, if one
has not dined well.

—Virginia Woolf

SET YOUR FEELINGS FREE

We know them for the fun they bring to the world, but even unicorns can run low on sparkle sometime—everyone feels sad from time to time, even if from the outside their lives might look glittery and magical.

If you find yourself feeling blue, don't hide away in a corner of the stable and bottle up those feelings. If you share your feelings with a trusted friend, family member, teacher, or colleague, you'll find your troubles become a little lighter. Maybe things won't look so bad once you've talked through what's making you sad, or else you may be able to come up with a way forward that makes things better, with their advice. Friends and family are the magical unicorns we need when we're going through tough times.

WHEN YOUR DAY NEEDS A BURST OF AWESOMENESS,

UNLEASH YOUR
INNER UNICORN!

When life looks like
it's falling apart, it
may just be falling
in place.

—Beverly Solomon

YOU ARE
LOVELY JUST
AS YOU ARE.

APPROACH YOUR WORK WITH FUN

It is a truth unicornically acknowledged that most of us have to go to school or work—unless we are full-time magical unicorns, of course. But it's not too hard bringing a bit of unicorn pizzazz to our working hours, with a little imagination.

Try bringing the most spangly multicolored notebooks and folders you can find to your office or classroom; decorating your notes and memos with stars, rainbows, and magical horseshoes; or ornamenting your desk with a bright and cheery bunch of flowers, if you can. You might need to play it a little safer for exam papers and official reports, but if you don't have to write in blue or black, break out the coloring pens and bring some rainbow magic into your daily life! You will have the Unicorn Seal of Approval if you do, and your paperwork will look truly out of this world.

I like
nonsense,
it wakes up the
brain cells.

—Dr. Seuss

YOU'RE ONE OF
A KIND. YOU'RE
A UNIQUORN.

DON'T FORGET
TO PLAY

If you come across a group of unicorns, you'll most likely find them playing "chase the rainbow" or "pin the silver lining on the cloud." That's because unicorns know how important it is to make time for fun and games. Our routines of work and study can make it seem sometimes as if there's no time to play, but we all need fun in our lives, whether we're five or ninety-five years old. Playing refreshes the spirit and lets us come back to our work with new energy and new ideas. Whether you choose to do a silly walk on your way to the bus stop, gargle the national anthem when you're cleaning your teeth, learn how to say all your friends' names backwards, or practice balancing a pencil on your nose (during a lesson or a meeting if you're feeling really brave), embrace the spirit of play and frolic like a unicorn!

UNICORN STYLE

How to shine, glitter, and
sparkle like a unicorn
every day

SHINE ON, YOU CRAZY UNICORN

There are as many unicorn fashion looks as there are unicorns, but one thing they all have in common is a tendency to sparkle. Unicorn fashion don't mean a thing if it ain't got that bling, so feel free to liven up your outfits with sequins, jewels, glitter, and every kind of twinkle you can get your hands on.

If you prefer a more restrained look, try sparkly shoes, a bespangled handbag, or a sequined bow in your hair. But why hold back? Even if you dressed as a disco ball from head to toe, you still wouldn't be OTT in a unicorn fashion parade.

Logic will get
you from A to B.
Imagination will
take you everywhere.

—Albert Einstein

YOU WEREN'T
BORN TO BE PERFECT.
YOU WERE BORN TO BE
A UNICORN—WHICH IS
PRETTY MUCH THE
SAME THING!

THESE COLORS ARE MADE FOR WEARING

Unicorns live in a magical rainbow land, and you can live there too just by bringing some red, orange, yellow, green, blue, indigo, and violet into your outfit. You can go big and bold: try color-blocking the full spectrum, from your hat down to your shoes, or wearing a rainbow-striped maxi dress. Or you can make a subtler statement with rainbow colors on your socks, belt, tie, or jewelry. Whichever approach you choose, you'll bring joy to everyone you meet, and you'll feel magical all day long.

Try to be
a rainbow
in someone's
cloud.

—Maya Angelou

THE UNICORNS
MADE ME DO IT.

WHITE CLOTHES ALWAYS WORK

Unicorns love to wear a rainbow, but for a simpler look, there's nothing like white. On a simmering sunny day, white keeps you cool and reflects the sunshine beautifully, and on a crisp wintry walk, a white outfit will make you friend to the snowy owl and snowman alike. Add some sparkly wings and you'll become an enchanting angelcorn!

IF A UNICORN SPARKLES IN A MAGICAL RAINBOW LAND AND NOBODY SEES IT,

IS IT STILL
AWESOME?
(YES.)

Accept no one's
definition of
your life;
define yourself.

—Harvey Fierstein

LET FREEDOM REIGN

Each new season, the fashion world brings new styles and shapes to the clothes in our high streets, and our magazines are full of tips on the latest new thing that we simply must wear if we want to stay in the cool crowd.

Unicorns love to strut, spring, pounce, and play, and the most important question to a unicorn fashionista is: do I feel happy when I wear this? If the answer is "Yay!" you know you've snagged a great fashion find. But if it's more of a "Neigh!" and you feel cooped up and uncomfortable, leave that outfit on the rails and trot away in search of more fun-filled pastures.

We ask ourselves,
"Who am I to be
brilliant, gorgeous,
talented, fabulous?"
Actually, who are
you not to be?

—Marianne Williamson

SHIMMY 'TIL YOUR SEQUINS SHIMMER!

PAINT YOURSELF
A RAINBOW

When it comes to fashion, it's not just your clothes and accessories that can be truly, madly unicorny —there are lots of other ways to sprinkle magical stardust all over your look.

With make-up, the only limit is your imagination: iridescent eyes, snow-frosted lipstick, and a sweep of rainbow highlighter across your cheekbones will show the world what you're made of. You can also apply stardust glitter to your face for an awesome out-of-this-world vibe.

You can be magical to the tips of your fingers and toes with multicolored sparkly nail polish, and why not add a tiny unicorn face so everyone knows you're a true believer?

Finally, hair color is the unicorn-lover's best friend. Whether you prefer a discreet panel or a full head of pastel shades, the world—and your hair—is now your oyster!

Don't let them tame you.

—Isadora Duncan

57

EVEN IF YOU
DON'T BELIEVE
IN SOME THINGS—
ALWAYS BELIEVE
IN YOURSELF.

TEAM UP WITH FASHION FRIENDS

Unicorns are indeed the most magical creatures on Earth, but they also have a whole host of friends who can't wait to reorganize your wardrobe! In the unicorn world, everyone who's fluffy, cute, or quirky is welcome. So instead of kitten heels on your feet, why not try a kitten print on your outfit? Or add some drama with a sassy llama print. Raid clothes stores, charity shops, and online retailers and craft stores for outfits bedecked with flamingos, cacti, zebras, koalas, or whatever else tickles your fashion fancy, and share their cuteness with the world.

UNICORN
POWER

How to make the most of
your unicorn strength, even
when things get tough

REMEMBER YOU
ARE AWESOME

It's all too easy to focus on what we think of as our faults—all those things that we've been told make us not quite good enough—but unicorns are perfect, and you are perfect, too, just the way you are.

To live a life full of unicorn joy, take time to stand in front of the mirror and notice all the things that are lovely about you. Your smile makes other people light up, so try smiling at yourself and see just how beautiful you are. The sparkle inside you is more important than any one detail of your appearance—so celebrate your sparkle, hold your head up high, and enjoy being the one and only, irreplaceable, wonderful you!

The more you are
like yourself, the
less you are like
anyone else, which
makes you unique.

—Walt Disney

WEIRD IS
WHAT AWESOME
LOOKS LIKE TO
NON-UNICORNS.

USE AFFIRMATIONS

Unicorns know that words are powerful, and have a magic all of their own. You can build some unicorn magic into your day by repeating affirmations to yourself, out loud if possible. Try one of these, or make up your own:

I am enough, and I am awesome
Today will be full of joy
I spread magic all around me
I believe in myself
I can do anything if I try!

You might feel self-conscious when you first start using affirmations, but in the world of unicorns, nothing is too silly to try, and everything has the possibility of magic in it.

The potential for greatness lives within each of us.

—Wilma Rudolph

EVEN IF YOU STOP
BELIEVING IN
UNICORNS, THEY
ALWAYS BELIEVE
IN YOU.

AWKWARD IS GOOD

When we're young—and, to be honest, even when we're older—we often feel that we have to fit in with the crowd, because the worst thing that could *possibly* happen would be to be different from everyone else. Well, the unicorns have got some news for you: different is good! Have you ever seen a unicorn try *not* to stand out? Exactly.

Whatever makes you feel different, whether you're nerdy, geeky, awkward, or simply unique in your own wonderful way, you are a magical unicorn, so show the world who you are, and never let anyone dull your sparkle. Your quirks are what make you extra special!

IF YOU'RE LUCKY ENOUGH TO STAND OUT FROM THE HERD,

DON'T EVER
CHANGE.

In order to
be irreplaceable
one must
always
be different.

—Coco Chanel

CELEBRATE DIFFERENCE
ALL AROUND YOU

Unicorns come in all shapes, sizes, patterns, and colors, and they're all magical. Just as you nurture and cherish the things that make you unique, make sure you've adjusted your vision so you can see those extraordinary qualities in the people all around you.

It's easy to put people in a box, or label them as "grumpy" or "mean," especially if you've had a tricky conversation with them, but everyone has a magical sparkly side if you just know where to look for it. Celebrate the good in the people you meet, and there will be more rainbows and loveliness for you and them.

A mind is like
a parachute.
It doesn't work if
it is not open.

—Frank Zappa

PRANCE LIKE NOBODY'S WATCHING!

SASHAY AWAY

In a perfect world, we would spend all our time sliding down rainbows, but every now and then life tries to poop on our parade, and it's up to us to choose how we respond. Unicorns are always polite and kind, but nobody walks all over them. When people are rude or have bad intentions, unicorns take a "talk to the hoof" approach, defending their position calmly yet firmly—and if a person won't listen to reason, it's absolutely OK to let them get on with it, and trot off to find a sunnier meadow to frolic in.

Unicorns can go anywhere, but they know how to set boundaries, and it's a great lesson to learn if you want to live a freer and more magical life.

There is just one
life for each of us:
our own.

—Euripides

KEEP YOUR
HEART OPEN
AND YOUR
TAIL SWISHY.

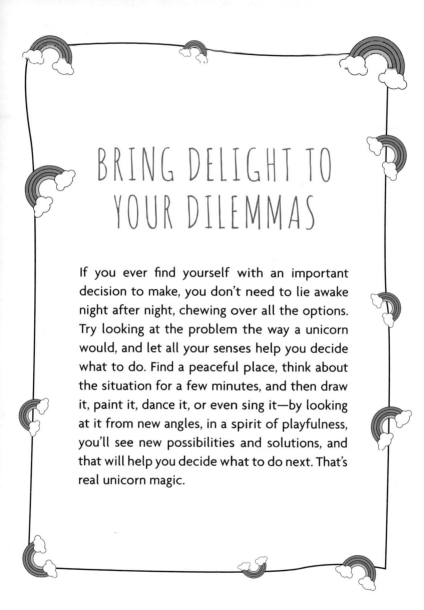

BRING DELIGHT TO YOUR DILEMMAS

If you ever find yourself with an important decision to make, you don't need to lie awake night after night, chewing over all the options. Try looking at the problem the way a unicorn would, and let all your senses help you decide what to do. Find a peaceful place, think about the situation for a few minutes, and then draw it, paint it, dance it, or even sing it—by looking at it from new angles, in a spirit of playfulness, you'll see new possibilities and solutions, and that will help you decide what to do next. That's real unicorn magic.

NEVER STOP DREAMING

How to keep bringing
unicorn magic into your
life—and how to share it
with the world

THE FUTURE BELONGS
TO THE UNICORNS

Unicorns believe that you should never give up on your dreams. We don't know where life is going to take us, but if we approach each day with a spirit of fantasy and enthusiasm, there's nothing we can't achieve.

One way to make your dreams more real, and therefore more achievable, is to write them down in a journal. Be as detailed or as vague as you like—just make sure you've made a note of the way you feel when you're thinking about all the magic the future holds for you. Include drawings or pictures from magazines if you like, and keep your journal somewhere easy to find, so you can dip into it whenever you need an inspiration boost.

If a little dreaming
is dangerous, the
cure for it is not
to dream less but
to dream more, to
dream all the time.

—Marcel Proust

DON'T STOP BELIEVING!

KEEP GOING

We all face big challenges in life from time to time, and sometimes it feels easier to give up when the road ahead of us is steep and difficult. Even unicorns, with their magical powers, find some mountains hard to climb, but just like us, they find their way to the top by taking each journey one rainbow-colored step at a time.

If your plans go wrong, go with them. A unicorn adapts to its surroundings with a swish of its twinkly tail, and you can do the same. *You* bring the magic to whatever next steps you take.

With perseverance and positivity no obstacle is too big—and with a unicorn trotting along cheerfully by your side, you'll reach your goal before you know it.

Tell me, what is it
you plan to do with
your one wild and
precious life?

—Mary Oliver

TURN YOUR
UNICAN'TS
INTO UNICANS.

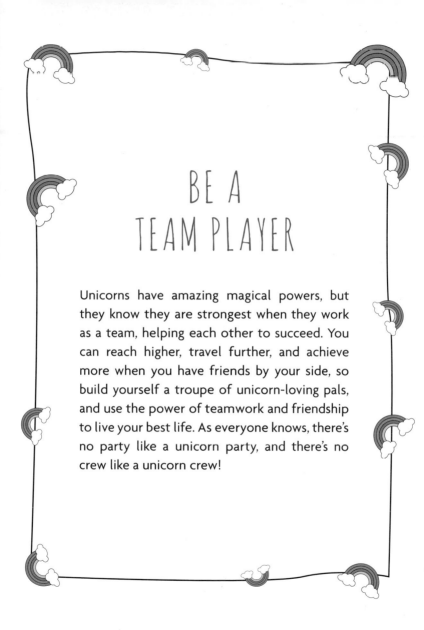

BE A
TEAM PLAYER

Unicorns have amazing magical powers, but they know they are strongest when they work as a team, helping each other to succeed. You can reach higher, travel further, and achieve more when you have friends by your side, so build yourself a troupe of unicorn-loving pals, and use the power of teamwork and friendship to live your best life. As everyone knows, there's no party like a unicorn party, and there's no crew like a unicorn crew!

UNICORNS
ARE AWESOME.
I AM AWESOME.

THEREFORE I AM
A UNICORN.

The best way
to cheer
yourself up
is to try to
cheer somebody
else up.

—Mark Twain

REST AND RECHARGE

It's a little-known fact that unicorns hibernate sometimes, when their magic banks need a boost. If you're feeling all out of sparkle, make time for some self-care. Your perfect pick-me-up might be a canter through the forest by yourself, with a soundtrack of birdsong and breezes rustling the leaves—or it might be a duvet day on the sofa, watching enchanting films, and eating your favorite snacks. Listen to your heart, give yourself some pampering, and when you're ready, bound out into the meadows again fully loaded with sparkles and sunshine.

Keep smiling
because life is a
beautiful thing and
there's so much to
smile about.

—Marilyn Monroe

WHEN IT
RAINS, LOOK
FOR RAINBOWS.
WHEN IT'S
DARK, LOOK
FOR STARS.

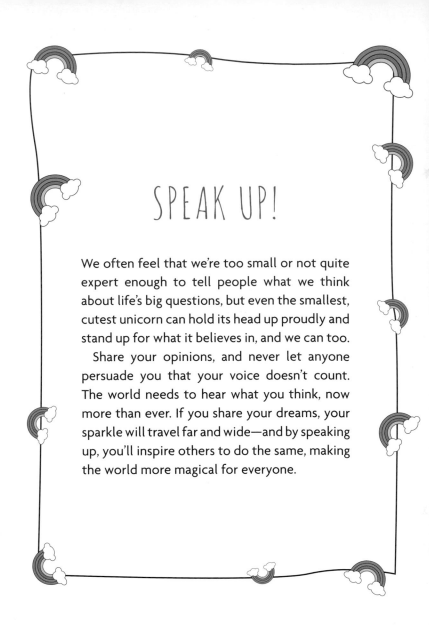

SPEAK UP!

We often feel that we're too small or not quite expert enough to tell people what we think about life's big questions, but even the smallest, cutest unicorn can hold its head up proudly and stand up for what it believes in, and we can too.

Share your opinions, and never let anyone persuade you that your voice doesn't count. The world needs to hear what you think, now more than ever. If you share your dreams, your sparkle will travel far and wide—and by speaking up, you'll inspire others to do the same, making the world more magical for everyone.

Beware, for I am fearless, and therefore powerful.

—Mary Shelley

BE THE UNICORN
YOU WISH TO SEE
IN THE WORLD.

MAKE THE WORLD
A BETTER PLACE

Unicorns believe in love and fairness, and they try every day to share the joys of life with those around them. Whether it's at school or work, with friends or family, in the place where you live or in the wider environment, there are positive steps you can take today to make things better. You might do this with a simple conversation, raising funds for a charity, volunteering with a local organization, or participating in a campaign that you care about. Whatever you choose, you'll be sharing your unicorn magic with the world, and making it better for everyone to live in.

IMAGE CREDITS